MW01533892

ZOOM FOR BEGINNERS

The Ultimate Guide to Master

Online Meetings and Webinars

Written by Colombo Publishing Company

© **Copyright 2020 by Colombo Publishing Company**
All rights reserved.

This document is geared towards providing exact and reliable information with regards to the topic and issue covered. The publication is sold with the idea that the publisher is not required to render accounting, officially permitted, or otherwise, qualified services. If advice is necessary, legal or professional, a practiced individual in the profession should be ordered.

- From a Declaration of Principles which was accepted and approved equally by a Committee of the American Bar Association and a Committee of Publishers and Associations.

In no way is it legal to reproduce, duplicate, or transmit any part of this document in either electronic means or in printed format. Recording of this publication is strictly prohibited and any storage of this document is not allowed unless with written permission from the publisher. All rights reserved.

The information provided herein is stated to be truthful and consistent, in that any liability, in terms of inattention or otherwise, by any usage or abuse of any policies, processes, or directions contained within is the solitary and utter responsibility of the recipient reader. Under no circumstances will any legal responsibility or blame be held against the publisher for any reparation, damages, or monetary loss due to the information herein, either directly or indirectly.

Respective authors own all copyrights not held by the publisher.

The information herein is offered for informational purposes solely, and is universal as so. The presentation of the information is without contract or any type of guarantee assurance.
The trademarks that are used are without any consent, and the publication of the trademark is without permission or backing by the trademark owner. All trademarks and brands within this book are for clarifying purposes only and are the owned by the owners themselves, not affiliated with this document

Table of Contents

INTRODUCTION

Zoom is a great and popular choice for web conferencing, with over one million meeting participants every day. Before the pandemic, many companies were already using the videoconferencing app Zoom for business meetings, interviews, and other purposes. More recently, many individuals facing long days without contact with friends and family have moved to Zoom for face-to-face and group get-togethers.

With much of the world now working from home during the Covid-19 crisis, many are turning to video calling

CHAPTER ONE:

GETTING STARTED ON ZOOM

Zoom

Zoom is a virtual conferencing platform that is easy to use. While the service was primarily aimed at enterprise consumers, it has become increasingly popular in the last couple of months, recording over 300 million daily users.

Zoom Meeting

What is a Zoom Meeting? Zoom Meetings are the foundation of Zoom, and the term refers to video conferencing meetings using the platform that allow remote and co-located meeting attendees to communication frictionlessly. Since you you don't need to have a Zoom account to attend a Zoom meetings, you can even meet with clients or conduct interviews with remote candidates virtually.

A "Zoom Meeting" simply refers to a meeting that's hosted using Zoom, and attendees can join the meeting in-person, via webcam or video conferencing camera, or via phone. For example, here's a photo of my team during a Zoom Meeting. We were all attending the meeting remotely, but sometimes, we attend the meeting via our company's conference room, where we pair Zoom with the Meeting Owl to create an inclusive meeting experience for all attendees.

Features of Zoom

1. Virtual Background

One of the features of zoom is VIrtual background. When using the app, one set background to avoid or hide cluttered background- a scope for eliminating distractions or highlighting branding. For setting the background, go to the setting and click on the virtual background.

2. Calendar Integration

Next in the line is calendar integration. In order to schedule a zoom online meeting in a fast and easiest way is to use free Zoom

Scheduler Extension or Plug-In for Outlook. These can be integrated into the existing calendaring system.

3. Waiting Room

One of the next impressive features of Zoom is its waiting room. Through the app, it is easy to see who comes into the meetings by enabling Waiting Room Feature. Also, admitting participants accordingly for security reasons can be made through the app. The host either admits one participant at a time or accepts everyone at once. The sending message feature is also available in the application.

4. Multi Sharing

A common similarity between Google Meet vs Zoom is sharing screens. Zoom's real-time collaboration can make participants share screens at the same time. Also, enabling the dual monitor's option through the Zoom settings allows viewing the two most recently shared screens side by side.

5. Personal Meeting Room

The next difference between features of Zoom vs Google Meet is a personal meeting room. Zoom's personal meeting ID (PMI) is reserved for having a virtual meeting room just for the host. Using it, the host can customize the PMI and room settings for serving better as per the meeting requirements.

6. Digital Touch Up

The next appealing feature of Zoom among many is digital touch up. Using the application one can touch up the digital appearance. By enabling Touch up My appearance, the soft focus is being laid to the entire screen. Through it, one can look more professional and polished.

When these were the features of Zoom, there are pros and cons of zoom reported by real users. Let's have a look at them too-

What Equipment Do I Need To Use Zoom

To use Zoom you will need one of the following:

- **Computer.** Windows or Apple computer with speakers and a microphone. (Note: Webcams are recommended but not required.)
- **Mobile Device.** iOS or Android
- **Phone.** Mobile device, desk, or landline

HD Cameras

These webcams work with Zoom on any Windows or Apple desktop or laptop computer.

- Logitech HD ConferenceCam
- Logitech HD Webcams
- VDO360 PTZ HD Camera
- VTEL HD3000PTZ Camera
- Vaddio Clearview USB
- Microsoft HD Webcams
- Freetalk HD Webcams
- Hovercam Solo 5 Document Webcam

USB Speaker Microphone All-in-One

These products are specially designed for Web conferencing with a Windows or Apple computer. You can plug these devices into any USB port on your computer.

- Jabra Speak 510

- Clearone Chat 150

- Logitech P710e

- Plantronics Calisto 600

- Phoenix Quattro3

- Voice Tracker Array

- Yamaha PSP-20UR

- Jabra USB Headphones

XLR Microphone Systems

These products are designed to work in auditoriums.

- Revolab Fusion Wireless Microphones

- Shure Wireless Conferencing System

- MXL Microphones for Conferencing

Downloading And Installing The Zoom Application

Zoom is a cloud based enterprise communications platform that provides video and audio conferencing, as well as, chat capabilities across mobile, desktop, and room

systems platforms.

To download and install the Zoom Application:

- Open your internet browser
- Go to https://zoom.us/download and from the Download Center, click on the Download button under "Zoom Client For Meetings".
    - ➤ This application will automatically download when you start your first Zoom Meeting.
- Once the download is complete, proceed with installing the Zoom application onto your computer

Registration For Zoom

How to sign up for the first time (WEB)

The first thing to do, of course, is to register for the service. You can do this either from your laptop or from your mobile phone. We'll cover the web service first.

- Start by going to zoom.us. You might first be asked to enter your date of birth. That's because if you are younger than 16, you aren't eligible to make a Zoom account unless it's for school.

- You'll next be presented with a few options for creating an account. At the top, you can enter your email in the box labeled "Your work email address." If you do this, move on to step two. Even though Zoom asks for a work email, a personal email should work fine.

- You can also create an account by clicking the "Sign in with Google" or "Sign in with Facebook" buttons, after which you just download the Zoom desktop app and move on to step seven.

- If you entered an email, Zoom will send an activation email to that address. Click the "Activate Account" button in the email or copy and paste the activation URL into your browser to activate your account.

- On the page that opens up in your web browser, you'll next be asked if you're signing up on behalf of a school. Assuming you aren't, click the "No" button and then click "Continue."

- On the next page, fill in your first and last name and a password.

- On the next page, you can invite other people to create a free Zoom account via email. You can skip this step if you want.

- Next, you'll be given a link to your personal meeting URL and will have the option to click an orange "Start Meeting Now" button to start a test meeting. If you copy that URL into your browser or click that orange button, you should be prompted to download the Zoom desktop app. Follow the prompts to install the app.

- After you've installed the Zoom app, you'll see buttons to "Join a Meeting" or "Sign In." To start your test meeting, click "Sign In."

- On the next screen, enter the email and password you just used to sign up for Zoom in your browser. If you registered using the "Sign in with Google" or "Sign in with Facebook" buttons, click those buttons here and follow the prompts.

- Once you're logged in, make sure you're on the "Home" tab, and then click the orange "New Meeting" button in the Zoom app. Your meeting will start.

For Mobile

If you sign up for Zoom using the mobile app, the process is similar to how it is on the web.

- Download the iOS or Android app. When you open the app for the first time, you'll be presented with the options to join a meeting, sign up for Zoom, or sign in to a Zoom account. Tap "Sign Up."

- You'll next be asked to confirm your age.

- Once you've done that, on the next screen, you'll be asked to enter your email address, and your first and last name. Once you do, "Sign Up" and you'll then be sent an activation email.

- Tap the "Activate Account" button in the email you receive, or copy and paste the activation URL into your mobile browser.

- From there, you'll be asked to complete the same steps outlined above to make an account, just from your mobile browser.

- Once you get to the screen that has your personal Zoom meeting URL and orange "Start Meeting Now" button, tap either and you'll be taken directly to a waiting room for your test meeting in the Zoom app.

- To open the meeting, tap the "Sign In" button at the bottom of the screen. On the next screen, enter your login information and tap the "Sign In" button.

- Your test meeting will open up in the app.

Preparing for a Zoom Meeting

Things you shouldn't do before a Zoom meeting and another 3 you should always do

DOS

#1: Do check your internet connection

If you're relying on Wi-Fi, make sure that everything is good before starting the meeting. I usually disconnect and reconnect and check the signal strength prior to a meeting. Speedtest.net is a good test, and you can check your results against Zoom's system requirements (which vary depending on what you're doing).

#2: Do check your speaker and mic

Buried in Zoom's Preference's is an Audio tab where you can test the mic and speakers. I suggest checking these before every meeting. Also, you can access more in-depth settings related to background noise suppression and echo cancellation by clicking on the Advanced button at the bottom of the screen.

#3: Check your video

Again, Zoom's Preference's screen is the place to do this -- click on Video. Look at the lighting and composition (no one wants to spend the whole meeting looking up your nose). Check the lighting (can people see you?) and also look for anything confidential or embarrassing that might be in the shot (especially if you move about).

If you plan to use a virtual background, check that this works properly prior to the start of the meeting (in the Zoom Preference's screen click on Virtual Background).

DON'TS

#1: Don't update Zoom or your OS immediately prior to a meeting

Yes, it's a good idea to keep Zoom updated, but I've had updates take a long time to download and install, I've had updates mess with settings, and I've had updates fail and leave me having to uninstall and reinstall Zoom. Same goes for operating system updates. Just leave them until after your meetings.

#2: Don't rely on your laptop's battery

If you're Zooming from a laptop, have it connected to the charger where possible. Video conferencing is very demanding on the hardware, and the last thing you want is to be left scrabbling for power.

#3: Don't have distractions on the screen

Facebook, Twitter, email and the like are all distractions, and people on the other end of the meeting will be able to tell if you are distracted by things.

Close anything that's not needed. Not only does that reduce on the potential for distraction, but it also means that you're less likely to have something pop up and make a noise. The quicker you get your meeting done, the quicker you can get back to other things!

How Do I Host A Video Meeting

Signing In

- Go to http://zoom.us and click on Sign In.

- You can use the "e-mail" and "password" that you have created, or use your Google (Gmail or Google App) or Facebook account to sign in with.

Note: If you do not have a current Zoom account, please click on Sign Up Free to create a new one.

Hosting a Meeting

- Open your Zoom app on your desktop and click Sign In.

- Log in using the E-mail and password that you have created, or with Google(Gmail), Facebook, or Login with SSO.

- Click the downward arrow and select Start with video, then click New Meeting to start an instant meeting.

How To Apply A Background In Zoom

If your workspace at home isn't quite so tidy, you can apply a background to virtually clean up the real clutter. It's like being a news anchor sitting in front of a green screen. Zoom's selection of landscapes can add a bit of whimsy to your meetings too.

Executives who need to portray a more professional appearance when doing video calls with clients can even upload their company's logo for use as a background, making it look like you're having the call in an actual conference room at work.

The feature is simple to use, and the camera on your handset or computer can apply the background even if you're not sitting in front of a green screen. Here's how to get start:

Step 1: Launch Zoom on your computer

Step 2: Go to the cogs button on the upper right-hand corner of your display to launch the Settings menu.

Step 3: Select Virtual Background in the left menu pane.

Step 4: After you do that, you can choose from a number of built-in background, like a scene from the beach, a view of San Francisco's iconic Golden Gate Bridge, or even the Aurora Borealis. A live preview will show how you will look in front of the background.

Step 5: To choose your own custom background, click on the + icon next to Choose Virtual Background. The option will let you upload your own custom video or photo for use as a virtual background. If you have a video of an aquarium, you can conduct your meeting in front of what would appear as a live fish tank, as an example. If you need inspiration for some fun animated backgrounds to use, Lightricks, the maker of popular photo editing app FaceTune, has uploaded some content to Dropbox that you can use.

Using a live background will reveal some artifacts around the edges, which can look choppy if you're moving around a lot during video calls. Additionally, virtual backgrounds shouldn't be used if you're planning on demonstrating or pointing to things with your hands — hands get canceled out with the use of virtual backgrounds. The background will appear more smooth if you're sitting in front of a green screen.

How To Share Screen Once On Zoom If You're Already On A Call

1. If you are already on a call, the process looks a bit different and may even be easier. From your call screen, click the "Share Screen" button. Whether you do so on your phone or computer, this button is found at the bottom center. Tap on your screen or move your cursor if this menu has disappeared. You can also use the SHIFT + COMMAND + S shortcut on your Mac or Alt + Shift +S on a PC.

2. On your desktop, this will open a pop-up with options. Select what you'd like to share and click the blue "Share" button to proceed.

3. This will automatically broadcast the app or desktop view you chose to share. A small Zoom pop-up will be visible at the top of the screen reminding you that you are broadcasting. If you hover over this pop-up you can find more options.

4. If you'd like to share a different screen, click the green "New Share" option in the middle. This will reopen the menu, where you

can switch apps or choose to use the whiteboard. In addition to the "New Share" option, you'll find other helpful buttons.

How To Record And Transcribe Your Zoom Call

If your business subscribes to a more advanced Zoom plan with cloud recording, you can record your meeting's audio to the cloud. Zoom's A.I. will help transcribe your meeting complete with timestamps and save the transcript as a .vtt text file. The meeting notes can be edited, if needed, for accuracy.

When you review your meeting video, there's even an option to display the transcription directly within the video, making it look like closed captioning.

Step 1: Open the Zoom web portal and sign in.

Step 2: Click on the Recordings tab on the left-hand side and choose Cloud Recordings. You'll need a premium Zoom account to use this feature, so you may have to inquire with your IT administrator or manager to see if your business is a subscriber.

Step 3: Enable Audio Transcript under Cloud Recordings, and save your changes.

Step 4: When you start a meeting, be sure to hit the Record button and choose Record to the Cloud.

Step 5: After the conclusion of the meeting, you'll receive an email alerting you that the transcript is ready.

Sign in and Join

After launching Zoom, click Join a Meeting to join a meeting without signing in. If you want to log in and start or schedule your own meeting, click Sign In.

How To Mute And Unmute Yourself

If you're not ready to speak when you join a Zoom meeting, or you just want to stay silent to keep a barking dog or chattering kids from being disruptive, you'll want to familiarize yourself with the mute button. If you're using audio routed through a computer or mobile device, look at the icons in the menu bar on the screen to see if you're muted or unmuted by default.

If you see a red slash over the microphone icon, you are muted. To turn the mute off, click the Unmute button at the bottom left corner of your meeting window. Other participants should be able to hear you just fine, as long as your audio is set up correctly. You can always switch to a different audio input during your meeting (a headset to your computer's built-in microphone, for example) by pressing the Audio Options button. You can also use this option to join in via phone while still connected to video on the computer client.

Starting your first meeting as the host

As the meeting host, there are several ways you can start your meeting. Your upcoming meetings will be listed in the Meetings tab of your Zoom desktop client or mobile app. You can click Start by the meeting name. You can also start your meetings from the Zoom web portal.

- Login to My Meetings.

- Under Upcoming Meetings, click Start next to the meeting you want to start.

- The Zoom client should launch automatically to start the meeting.

Inviting Others To Join Your Meeting

Inviting others to join your meeting is as simple as sharing the invitation or join link.

The short answer is: you must do so manually. There are two ways to do this: through calendar invites, or via your own email account.

If you wish to invite others through a calendar, links to Google Calendar, Outlook Calendar, and Yahoo Calendar are displayed once your meeting has been saved.

Alternatively, next to the "join URL" link on this screen, there is an option to "copy this invitation."

Clicking on this page element brings up a screen with all of the important information required for the meeting, including the URL, of which the meeting ID is already embedded. Copy this to your clipboard, open your email client, paste the details into a new message, and invite away.

So, in short, all participants need is the meeting URL, date and time, and a password if applicable.

If you want to try out features before bringing other people in, create a test meeting at this stage and select "Start this meeting." Alternatively, you can do exactly the same within the first page of the Zoom desktop app:

The first prompt, in either case, will ask you to join with computer audio if you are on PC, and will also give you the option to test your speaker and microphone. At the top right of the meeting window, you can choose to go full screen.

We are now going to go over the basic settings you need to know about in meetings for management purposes.

Two fundamental options can be found in the bottom-left part of the black menu tab: the option to mute/unmute your microphone and either start/stop your camera. If you are using an external microphone, speaker, or camera, open up the arrow tabs next to these options to choose which equipment you want to use (external or inbuilt).

Moving on, the "Manage Participants" tab is particularly important. Under this tab, you can find "invite," which is useful if you've forgotten to bring someone into a session.

Clicking this option will bring up a box with everyone connected to the meeting. If you hover over a name, you can mute/unmute them, and at the bottom, there are options for doing the same for every participant. In the interests of privacy, however, hosts and other participants cannot control individual camera feeds.

A handy feature to note here under "More" is "lock," which stops anyone else from joining an active session.

Speaker or Gallery view: At the top, you can pick one of two view options -- but this only impacts how you view a meeting, and not others. By default, Active Speaker is the default video layout -- in which the person talking is ramped up to a larger screen -- but there is also a gallery layout which brings in every participant on one screen through a form of grid.

The "Share Screen" tab has a number of interesting features. When selected, under "Basic," you can choose to share your PC screen with others, including your full desktop, browser, or open applications. There is also a whiteboard option that can be annotated -- we will talk about this more shortly -- and it is possible to share iPhone screens if you are on the move, too.

Under "Advanced," you can share a screen portion, music or sound only, or content from a second, connected camera.

There is also a file-sharing tab under "share screen" (shown under "Files"), which includes application links to Dropbox, Microsoft OneDrive, Google Drive, and Box.

As a host, you can also use the arrow next to the "Share Screen" tab to control whether participants are limited to one screen share at a time, or alternatively, you can give permission for multiple screens to be shared at once.

Now, let's talk about messaging. The "Chat" tab on the main bar is designed for users to type out questions and messages, as well as share files either hosted by cloud storage providers or stored directly on your PC.

As a host, you can also select the "..." button to save a chat session and control who participants can talk to -- no one, the host alone, everyone publicly, or everyone publicly and privately.

The final tab of note is the "Record" option, which you may want to use if you are discussing work matters and want to save the session in order to email a copy of it to others later. By default, no one except the host can record a session unless the host gives permission to do so. (More: Check out TechRepublic's guide to recording Zoom meetings.)

Finally, the "End Meeting" tab finishes the session. If the host needs to leave but the meeting should carry on, they can assign the host status to another participant -- but enabling co-hosts has to be selected first in the "Meetings" tab and can only be selected by subscription holders. Alternatively, you can leave the meeting or end the meeting for all.

How To Enable And Add A Co-Host

The co-host feature allows the host to share hosting privileges with another user, allowing the co-host to manage the administrative side of the meeting, such as managing participants or starting/stopping the recording. The host must assign a co-host. There is no limitation on the number of co-hosts you can have in a meeting or webinar.

Co-hosts do not have access to the following controls as they are only available as host controls in a meeting:

- Start closed captioning and assign someone or a third-party to provide closed captioning
- Start live streaming
- End meeting for all participants
- Make another participant a co-host
- Start breakout rooms or move participants from one breakout room to another
- Start waiting room (co-hosts can place participants in waiting room or admit/remove participants from the waiting room)

Co-hosts also cannot start a meeting. If a host needs someone else to be able to start the meeting, they can assign an alternative host.

Note: By default, meetings hosted by On-Prem users with on-premise meeting connectors, can not assign co-host rights to another participant. This option must be enabled by Zoom support.

To enable the Co-host feature for all members of your organization:

- Sign into the Zoom web portal as an administrator with the privilege to edit Account settings, and click Account Settings.

- Navigate to the Co-host option on the Meeting tab and verify that the setting is enabled. If the setting is disabled, click the Status toggle to enable it. If a verification dialog displays, choose Turn On to verify the change.

- (Optional) If you want to make this setting mandatory for all users in your account, click the lock icon, and then click Lock to confirm the setting.

Group

To enable the co-host feature for all members of a specific group:

- Sign into the Zoom web portal as an administrator with the privilege to edit User groups, and click Group Management.

- Click the name of the group, then click the Settings tab.

- Navigate to the Co-host option on the Meeting tab and verify that the setting is enabled. If the setting is disabled, click the Status toggle to enable it. If a verification dialog displays, choose Turn On to verify the change.

Note: If the option is grayed out, it has been locked at the account level, and needs to be changed at that level.

- (Optional) If you want to make this setting mandatory for all users in this group, click the lock icon, and then click Lock to confirm the setting.

User

To enable the co-host feature for your own use:

- Sign into the Zoom web portal and click My Meeting Settings (if you are an account administrator) or Meeting Settings (if you are an account member).
- Navigate to the Co-host option on the Meeting tab and verify that the setting is enabled.
- If the setting is disabled, click the Status toggle to enable it. If a verification dialog displays, choose Turn On to verify the change.

Note: If the option is grayed out, it has been locked at either the Group or Account level, and you will need to contact your Zoom administrator.

Using co-host in a meeting

There are two ways that you can make a user a co-host.

During a meeting:

- Hover over a user's video.
- Click the more icon
- Click Make Co-Host.

Using the participants window:

- Click on Manage Participants in the meeting controls at the bottom of the Zoom window.
- Hover over the name of the participant who is going to be a co-host, and choose More.
- Click Make Co-Host.
- Once a participant has been made a co-host, they'll have access to the co-host controls.

Controlling and disabling in-meeting chat

As the host, you can control which meeting or webinar participants are allowed to chat with. You can also disable the chat for all participants or disable private chat, so participants cannot send private messages

Controlling chat access

Meeting and webinar hosts can control whether participants can chat with everyone, with panelists and the host (for webinars), or only with the host.

- Start a meeting or webinar as host.
- Click Chat in the Meeting Controls.
- At the bottom of the in-meeting Zoom Group Chat window, click More, and then choose an option for Allow attendees to chat with.
  - ➢ For meetings, the host can allow attendees to chat with everyone or with the host only.

> ➤ For webinars, the host can allow attendees to chat with no one, with all panelists (including host), or with all panelists and attendees.

Disabling in-meeting chat

You can turn chat for all of your meetings and webinars from your Profile Settings, if you do not want to use the chat in your meetings and webinars. This will prevent the host, co-hosts, and participants from chatting for any meetings you host. The Chat option will no longer appear in the Meeting Controls.

You can disable the Private Chat, which will prevent participants from sending messages to individuals instead of the entire group.

- Sign in to the Zoom web portal.
- In the navigation menu, click Settings.
- Click the Chat and Private Chat toggles to disable in-meeting chat.
- Click Save Changes

How To Generate Meeting Reports For Registration And Polling

If your Zoom meeting has registration or polling enabled, you can generate a registration or polling report for further analysis. The registration report contains the following information of registered participants:

- First and last name

- Email address

- Date and time of registration

- Approval status

The polling report contains the following information of participants that answered a poll question:

- Username and email address

- Date and time they submitted their answer

- The poll question and the participant's answer

Note:

- Meeting reports are automatically deleted 30 days after the scheduled date. This is also when the meeting is removed the from the Previous Meetings page in the web portal.

- If you delete a meeting from your Meetings list in the web portal, you cannot generate reports for that meeting. You can still download any reports you generated before deleting the meeting.

- You should generate meeting reports after your meeting has ended. If generated a report before starting the meeting, you should re-generate the report to obtain the data collected during the meeting.

Instructions

- Sign in to the Zoom web portal.
- Navigate to Account Management > Reports.
- In the Usage Reports tab, click Meeting.

A list of upcoming and previous meetings will be generated. You can search by time range or by meeting ID.

- Next to Report Type, select the Registration Report or Poll Report.

- In the drop-down menu below Report Type, select one of these options:

  ➢ Search by time range: Select a time range then click Search.

  ➢ Search by meeting ID: Enter the meeting ID and click Search.

- Click Generate in the last column. You can also use the check boxes to select multiple meeting then click Generate at the top.

Zoom will redirect you to the Report Queues tab where you can download the report as a CSV file.

CHAPTER TWO:

ZOOM VS OTHER CONFERENCING TOOLS

Zoom Vs Facebook Room

Messenger room: Any Facebook user can create a room, either from the Facebook Messenger app or through Facebook itself. The host can then send the invite link to participants and have them join. Alternatively, the host can directly add users residing in their Facebook contacts. Once added to a room, participants can come and go as they wish, as long as the room is still functioning. Only the host has the option to shut down a room.

Zoom meeting: These are more traditional in that a host creates a meeting and invites participants. Once the meeting ends, all participants are automatically kicked out of the room. Unlike Messenger Rooms, once the call ends, participants cannot re-enter the room and the invite link expires.

Number of Participants

There are a lot of video conferencing apps, but not all can accommodate a big number of participants. In this case, both Zoom and Facebook Messenger Rooms are excluded. However, the number of participants that Zoom can accommodate is twice the number of participants that Messenger Rooms can. Rooms will soon hold up to 50 people with no time limit.

Cost

Here's another thing to consider if you are still thinking about what to choose between Facebook Messenger Rooms vs Zoom. Rooms allow users to use all of its features for free. Contrary to Messenger Rooms, if you use Zoom, to be able to access all of its features, upgrading to their pro version is needed

Zoom Vs Google Meet

Zoom is a video conferencing platform for businesses founded in 2011. It boasts HD video, conference rooms, and voice and text chat available under a number of pricing packages. Zoom is also used by educational institutions, governments, and non-profit organizations to conduct meetings.

Features

HD Video and Audio with support for up to 1000 video participants.

Text Chat: Message team members before, during, and after meetings.

Unique Video Call Features: Add a custom video background, conduct polls and Q&A in call, and enable virtual hand raising.

Dial-In Options: Participants can dial-in to meetings. Option to automatically call any participant's phone when the meeting starts.

Breakout Rooms: Split your Zoom meeting into up to 50 different sessions for group discussion.

Meeting Recording: Record your meetings and store them locally or on the cloud.

Screen Sharing: Multiple callers can share their screens at the same time. Team members can also annotate each others' screens.

GCM Encryption: In the last few months, Zoom has received numerous complaints of outsiders hacking into meetings and sharing sensitive content. As such, Zoom has made it a priority to strengthen its security system. The result is new AES 256-bit GCM Encryption that will protect meetings from interference and secure meeting data.

Conference Rooms: Host or join Zoom meetings directly from existing conference room systems. They can also be optimized to the size of your conference room.

Integrations: Connect Zoom with hundreds of other apps such as Slack, Microsoft Teams, and Google Calendar. Invite team members through other apps and add your meetings to your calendar.

Google Meet is the successor to Google Hangouts. It can be accessed by individuals for free and as part of Google's G Suite collection for businesses that includes access to Google Drive, Docs, and a custom domain Gmail. Google Meet offers video, audio, and text chat for anyone with a Google account.

Features

Unlimited Meetings with up to 100 participants for free or 250 for businesses using G Suite.

Text Chat: Message team members during meetings.

Live Captioning: Add live closed captions to video calls (English only).

Screen Sharing: Present your entire screen or a single application window to other meeting participants.

Noise Cancellation: Coming soon, this feature will cancel most extraneous noise in meetings. For a preview of this exciting feature, check out this video.

Dial-In Options: Both US and International numbers can dial-in to meetings.

Cloud Recording and Storage: Record and store your calls on Google Drive.

Security: Google Meet includes numerous security features such as encryption both in transit and at rest, 2FA, Advanced Protection Program Enrollment, and DLP for Google Drive storage.

Integrations: Google Meet integrates with Google products such as Gmail, Google Drive, Google Calendar, and Google Classroom. G Suite includes additional integrations with work productivity apps like Slack, Freshdesk, and Trello.

Meeting Time, Participants limit

Google Meet is arriving for free to everyone in the coming weeks. Likewise, Zoom already has a free version. But just like other freemium offerings, the free versions of Google Meet and Zoom both have some limitations. Google Meet will offer a meeting limit of 60 minutes for free users. This means that you can't hold a virtual meeting for more than 60 minutes if you're using the free version. However, the time limit isn't in place until September 30. Zoom, on the other hand, provides a 40 minutes limit on group meetings under its free option.

On the part of participants limit, both Google Meet and Zoom let you host up to 100 participants for each of your virtual meetings.

Interface

Zoom is popular for its Gallery view that displays up to 49 participants on a single screen. However, Google Meet recently mimicked that interface by enabling an expanded tiled layout that simultaneously shows up to 16 participants at once. Google also recently added a low-light mode that uses artificial intelligence (AI) to adjust video on the basis of lighting conditions. The feature is initially limited to mobile users, though.

Recording

Zoom allows you to record meetings in MP4 (video) and M4A (audio) formats that you can store locally on your system. This is unlike Google Meet that doesn't allow recording of virtual meetings for free users. However, if you're a paid G Suite Enterprise or G Suite Enterprise for Education editions, you can record meetings seamlessly. Notable, the recording support will be available for free users until September 30 on Google Meet.

Availability

Since video conferences are no longer limited to desktops and laptops, both Google Meet and Zoom are available for mobile devices based on Android and iOS. Google Meet is also accessible directly through Chrome and other modern browsers and doesn't require any additional plugins. You just need to visit meet.google.com to host a meeting. Similarly, you can participate in a scheduled meeting by visiting its link in your eligible browser. This isn't the case with Zoom as it doesn't allow you to host a meeting through a browser. Nevertheless, you can join a meeting via your browser. There are also plugins for Google Chrome and Mozilla Firefox that you can use to schedule your meeting.

Emojis & GIFs

Zoom is not that flexible with emojis but it does let you use GIFs. Zoom web conferencing allows admins the ability to turn on and off. Furthermore, Zoom's whiteboard capabilities allow one to draw on different slides and screens.

On the other hand, Google hangouts let users search for and use a plethora of emojis (animated and unanimated) along with GIFs. One can use them during the chats anytime required.

Zoom Vs Skype

Zoom and Skype are two of the most recommended communication tools.

You can use both platforms to hold video calls, chat, and host meetings or webinars. And if you're seeking a new platform to help you do these things, you're likely considering both platforms.

Overall, there may not seem to be huge differences between Zoom and Skype. But the decision to implement one over another can still have a significant impact on your team. From our experience as a remote team, we know each platform fits different needs.

Zoom

Zoom is no ordinary video communication platform. It's a cloud-based innovative technology that houses a full spectrum of modern conferencing tools. Zoom comes with breakout sessions, which you can leverage to split your viewers (for instance clients or employees) into smaller groups for webinar trainings, specific topics or online class discussions. With Zoom, the organizer has the power to fully control the meeting. You can mute all microphones, control attendees' presentation access and so on. Moreover, this tool allows attendees to contribute to the conversation by virtually raising their hands.

Zoom's chat utility also lets viewers directly communicate with the instructor and other attendees, ensuring a collaborative classroom setting.

Skype

Imagine communication with your employees via instant messaging, screen sharing, file sharing, as well as informal video or audio calls right from your PC/phone. Effective and direct — that's what Skype is all about. With a wide user base, chances are that your employees are already familiar with it. Skype is designed using innovative technology for easy communication.

Like Zoom, Skype's intuitive chat interface allows users to send quick messages to other users. Users can effortlessly integrate video with audio right from their chat windows. In a nutshell, Skype is a great platform for instant messaging, document sharing, screen sharing and informal-based video or audio calls.

Using Zoom, you can:

- Conduct live video chat.

- Access meeting analytics, such as top users by meeting minutes.

- Easily screen-share during a call.

- Use the recording feature to save and document your sessions.

- Hold brainstorming sessions with Zoom's on-screen whiteboard feature.

- Access in-depth support, such as live help, online chat, phone support, FAQs, help articles, and video tutorials.

- Hook up integrations such as Slack and Zapier.

- Start using for free, as Zoom's free plan lets you host up to 100 participants in a video call.

You can also use Zoom to run webinars. Using a custom registration URL, you can invite attendees to your webinar in Zoom. Thanks to Zoom's recording feature, you can also save your webinar and reuse it again.

With Skype, you can:

- Use IM, hold video chats, and make local, domestic, and international calls.

- Conduct both screen and document sharing that supports large files.

- White-board, post a poll, and hold a Q&A session.

- Start with the free version, which works well for smaller teams.

Zoom vs. Cisco Webex

Video Quality

Independent tests show that Zoom has superior video quality in HD. Your colleagues and clients don't want their software to be the reason they see a grainy, choppy video. While Webex also has high-quality video, Zoom has the edge here again.

Capacity

When it comes to video conferencing solutions, nothing takes center stage quite like the capacity to accommodate users. While Webex can accommodate up to 200 people, Zoom can accommodate up to 1000 users per one web or video conferencing session with an Enterprise plan.

Conference Features

Both platforms have similar qualities when it comes to conference features. For instance, Webex is synonymous with its ability to support co-browsing, remove attendees and allow file transfers — tasks you can also perform in Zoom Video Conferencing. Additionally, Zoom offers a unique feature called Break-Out Sessions. When shopping around for a software that can take your video conferencing experience to the next level, choose a conference solution packed with features that suit your individual business needs.

Security Features

Security is important — especially for business meetings and video conferencing sessions. Both Webex and Zoom offer solutions that are highly secure and reliable.

Features such as encryption and user authentication optimize the security of both video conferencing platforms. What's more, both offer security control when it comes to desktop sharing. Both encrypt meetings, transmission and storage. For Zoom's Telehealth solution, they can also include HIPPA compliant security for patient to doctor communications.

Meeting Follow-Up

For any business, meeting follow-ups are extremely important. This allows participants to view the previous meeting's recording and listen to them again whenever they need. Zoom is outfitted with a unique Participant Reporting feature that checks all the members who reported at the meeting. In Webex, this feature isn't available.

User-Friendly Design

When it comes to business software, user-friendliness and ease-of-use are two important factors you should seriously consider. Complex software wastes time. Based on consumer feedback, Zoom is more user-friendly as compared to Webex. Zoom allows users to instantly join an online video conference or meeting, with common features across all devices. So, no matter what device you're using, you'll always be able to enjoy all its great features. Webex requires a more lengthy registration and checkin process compared to Zoom. With Zoom you're into your meeting faster.

Pricing

Pricing is a fundamental aspect when it comes to choosing a dependable video conferencing platform for your business. Companies tend to go for cost-effective and flexible tools that allow them to scale whenever the need arises. If features are relatively similar, the cost is a great tiebreaker.

When compared to Webex, Zoom historically offered much more affordable pricing. But in response to Zoom, Webex recently enhanced their free plan. While Webex's top business plan comes in at $26.95 per month, Zoom only charges hosts no more than $19.99 per month per user for a business account and offers a free plan for up to 100 participants. Even at that low price, Zoom offers unique features and high-quality video and sound. What's more, (unlike Webex) Zoom offers a free trial period for new users through partners like DGI.

Zoom vs Bluejeans

Zoom is a business that specialises in video conferencing – but that isn't all it does. There are plenty of other features to explore too, including simple and accessible interfaces that make users feel confident with their new UC set-up. They can even provide solutions for employee training, online meetings, and video webinars for your next industry event. One of the more recent products available from Zoom, the "Zoom Room" has also seen significant adoption.

Like Zoom, BlueJeans also specialises in the world of video conferencing, offering services like online video meetings, huddle rooms, and event support. BlueJeans also offers social broadcasting features, which allows users to cast content into social media. BlueJeans is a leader in their field, offering a diverse range of services and packages to customers from all backgrounds.

Meeting Room Products

Both Zoom and BlueJeans seem to excel at transforming the meeting room space. Whether you're looking for a small huddle-room solution or something larger, you can find the immersive video and audio conferencing services you need with either one of these vendors.

BlueJeans Meetings

BlueJeans Meetings is a simple, and effective way for companies to access enterprise-grade video calls with the support of high-definition Dolby audio. Users can connect instantly with customers and coworkers on any mobile device, conference room system, or laptop. BlueJeans Meetings also offers features like:

One-Click Scheduling: With one click, you can add a video call to any Outlook or Google calendar, without entering codes, passwords, or conference IDs

Screen Sharing and Collaboration: Share your latest documents and video clicks instantly or share your entire screen

Dolby Voice Audio: High-quality, high-definition sound with automatic background noise cancellation

Simple Integrations: Boost productivity with a range of integrations to Skype for Business, Workplace, and Slack

Cloud Streaming and Recording: Record and share meetings including audio, video, and documentation

Verified security: Ensure security with a range of safe deployment options

Room compatibility: Users can join meetings from Polycom, Cisco, Lifesize, and a selection of other SIP-based room software services

Zoom Meetings

Described as the ultimate video conferencing and web conferencing service, Zoom has achieved a fantastic Meeting room solution for their customers. he Zoom Meetings product includes:

Online Meeting Services: HD audio and video support for up to 500 video participants, with screen sharing and collaboration, features built-in

Training services: Solutions for co-annotation and whiteboarding, as well as an attention indicator device to keep meeting participants focused

Technical support: Easy start and join features, remote screen control features and more

Integrated scheduling: Zoom works with a customer's in-built scheduling system, including work emails, mobile scheduling, and more

Room Products

"Rooms" are emerging as a more popular solution for the meeting room space, as companies look for ways to connect everything they need in a conference environment, including whiteboarding, connectivity, and video collaboration. Both Zoom and BlueJeans offer their own unique "Rooms" services:

BlueJeans Rooms

The BlueJeans Rooms product is intended to help companies transform any business space into a fully-immersive conference room with video and audio support. BlueJeans Rooms allow connections with people on any SIP conference room system, as well as users on mobile or desktop devices, these Rooms also include:

Wireless screen sharing features: Show off your laptop screen anywhere in the conference room

Google and Microsoft Calendar Integration: Establish follow-up meetings that suit everyone's schedule

Universal setup features: The simple user interface comes with easy-to-read instructions and wrap-up reminders, so there's no training required

Central management: Customers can remotely monitor any room in their BlueJeans network and identify issues with a live moderator console

Support services: Extend the scale of an IT department with the BlueJeans team of global conferencing experts

Zoom Rooms

Based entirely on software, Zoom offers a highly scalable and innovative room experience, complete with integrated audio features, flawless video systems, and wireless content sharing solutions. Some of the features included with Zoom Rooms include:

Integration with anyone: Anyone can get access to HD video and audio through desktop, mobile, and other conference system devices

Wireless sharing: There's no need for dongles and cables, you can simply present content wirelessly from a device or laptop

One-touch meeting starts: Use voice commands and one-touch meetings to start scheduled conferencing or instant messaging on your calendar system

Overview and management: View and manage your conference rooms from a single user interface

Native Integration: Zoom offers easy integration with the Crestron Mercury system for speakers, tablet connectivity, and microphone performance all-in-one

Plans and Pricing

The software offered by Zoom and BlueJeans on a basic subscription level are similar in a lot of ways. After all, both companies are devoted to offering their customers high-performance audio and video conferencing solutions within a diverse meeting room environment. Of course, one of the ways that customers can more easily choose the service that's right for them is to look at the pricing and package services available. For instance:

BlueJeans Packages and Pricing

BlueJeans offers a range of three different pricing and package options, including:

Me: The system for small businesses and individuals, this product is available for £9.99 per host per month, and it allows for meetings with up to 50 participants, connections from any computer or mobile device, and unlimited meeting durations. There's also access to high-definition Dolby audio

My Team: Designed for mid-sized companies, this £13.32 package allows for meetings of up to 75 participants, and comes with cloud meeting recording, a command centre dashboard, and historical meeting analytics. Users can also integrate My Team with HipChat, Skype for Business, and Slack

My Company: Optimised for the enterprise environment, My Company offers meetings for up to 100 participants, along with room system calendar support, custom branding features, and unlimited cloud reporting. There's also a service for live meeting control and monitoring

Zoom Packages and Pricing

One area where Zoom differs from its competitors is in its packaging options. Zoom has a basic "free" version available to customers, while many other businesses don't offer the same service. Zoom's packages include:

Basic: This is the free version of Zoom, which hosts up to 100 participants, offers group meetings for up to 40 minutes, and online support. There are unlimited 1-on-1 meetings available, and there is also no limit on how many meetings you can host

Pro: Available for £11.99 per month, per host, the Pro version of Zoom comes with all the basic features, plus unlimited meeting duration, admin features, user management, reporting, and 1GB of cloud recording

Business: For small to mid-sized companies, the "Business" package is available for £15.99 a month, and includes dedicated phone support, a vanity URL, an admin dashboard, and the option for on-premise deployment

Enterprise: Designed specifically for the larger enterprise, this package is available for £15.99 per month, per host, and includes 200 participants, unlimited cloud storage, and a dedicated success manager. There's also the option for bundle discounts on Zoom Rooms and Webinars

Microsoft Teams Vs Zoom

Microsoft Teams is a collaboration tool designed to improve internal communication.

Zoom is a web conferencing software that facilitates high-performance video and audio conferencing both internally and externally.

Microsoft Teams is a popular choice for businesses that use Office 365 products. It is packaged in with the Office 365 suite and syncs up well with other Microsoft technologies. Zoom is used by companies that are looking for high-quality video conferencing that is easy to set up for both employees and external users.

Some companies make use of both Microsoft Teams and Zoom. These companies use Microsoft Teams for its chat features and its integrations with Office 365 and use Zoom for all their web conferencing.

Features

Microsoft Teams and Zoom both provide web conferencing features, but also have unique features that set them apart.

Microsoft Teams includes a robust chat service that allows users to communicate quickly without setting up a conference. Syncing with Office 365 also makes collaboration easy by allowing file sharing and calendar support. Microsoft's feature set is focused around perfecting internal communication.

Zoom is focused on video and audio conferencing. Zoom makes for easy conferencing even with users that are not part of the company account. Zoom also provides features such as multiple screen sharing to support web-based presentations. Lastly, Zoom web conferences boast high-quality video and audio.

Limitations

Microsoft Teams and Zoom both provide strong features in their area of expertise, but they also have some limitations that can impact their effectiveness.

Microsoft Teams loses some of its utility if a business is not using the Microsoft suite of office software. This is important to consider as Microsoft Teams also lacks many third-party integrations. Additionally, Microsoft Teams is missing some advanced conferencing features like multiple screen share.

Zoom has powerful web conferencing features but is missing some of the collaboration features that Microsoft Teams has, such as the chat feature. Zoom also experiences some performance issues with international conferences if the connection is less than perfect. Lastly, The free pricing plan for Zoom has a time limit of 40 minutes on group conferences.

Pricing

Both Microsoft Teams and Zoom offer a free version of their software with limited functionality.

Microsoft Teams is included in Office 365, which has three tiers of pricing. The cheapest option is $5.00 per user per month and includes a small number of Office services including Teams and SharePoint. The Office 365 Business Premium plan costs $12.50 per user per month and includes the Microsoft Office Suite (Word, Excel, etc.). Lastly, the Microsoft 365 Business Plan costs $20.00 per user per month and includes advanced security protection. All Microsoft Team's plans require a one year commitment.

Zoom's Pro pricing tier costs $15.00 per host per month and allows meetings as long as 24 hours. The business tier costs $20.00 per host per month and includes custom branding. Lastly, the enterprise tier costs $20.00 per host per month and requires at least 50 hosts. This plan includes unlimited cloud storage.

UX (User Interface)

The user interface and experience are truly where Zoom excels in the Microsoft Teams vs Zoom debate. Zoom users all rave over its simple interface and the ability to get end-users up and running with little to no training or IT support.

Microsoft Teams poses a bigger challenge as users need to get up to speed on how to interact in different channels and Teams, incorporate file sharing, and also all of the other Office 365 applications baked into Teams. Although the full set of workstream collaboration functionality built into Teams clearly allows it to offer a broader surface area of usage and scenarios (and hence a better value) than Zoom, this precise value is also in some ways its Achilles heel with respect to onboarding.

Room Systems

As parts of the Zoom vs Teams battleground threaten to become increasingly commoditized, one area of unique differentiation is the "room systems" installed in an organization. A room system can range from a simple huddle room configuration all the way up to a deluxe executive conference room. In our webinar on UC Conference Rooms: The Good, the Bad, and the Ugly, we break down everything you need to know about room systems, including comparing Microsoft Teams vs Zoom room systems. While both offer device management, touch enhancements, companion experiences with mobile, and dual-screen rooms support, Zoom has the added benefit of people counting, and Teams has proximity detection. Another difference between Zoom vs Microsoft Teams is that Zoom certifies both integrators and hardware providers while Teams only certifies the hardware solutions.

Integrations

Integrations are a huge part of WSC platforms and Zoom has also made them a core part of their offering as well for the UCaaS space. The integrations (or app store add-ons) enhance and broaden the utility of the platform and help end-users become even more productive while using the platform. Many younger users already have an app store mentality, meaning they are quick to find and applications that help make their day-to-day easier and more efficient. This is another big factor in the Microsoft Teams vs Zoom debate.

Microsoft Teams' biggest win is its close, baked-in integration of Office 365 apps, but beyond that, there are over 70 integrations for Microsoft Teams that include options for ticket management, surveys, weather, news, etc.

In Microsoft's case, integrations are typically to bring app data into its own platform. On the flip side, Zoom is often added as an integration to other platforms. A great example of this is how Zoom and Slack work together. In addition to the Slack integration, Zoom has over 100 integrations, including an integration with Office 365.

Zoom vs ezTalks

Zoom – Zoom is a well-known video conferencing solution that can be helpful for both large and small businesses. It can help enhance your communication in various ways. Zoom offers you a great number of features with the help of which you can enjoy call clarity, group collaboration and seamless integration with business applications. Using the conferencing service you can record conferences, share your screen, annotate collaboratively, and enjoy a lot more.

ezTalks is a cloud-based video conferencing software which enables SMBs & large enterprises to communicate & collaborate instantly online via HD video & audio

ezTalks vs Zoom Comparison:

Features

The tool that you choose should support the processes, workflows, reports and needs that matter to your team. When it comes to this, it's important to consider their features & functionality. Then, we'll compare ezTalks with Zoom based on some prominent features.

ezTalks:

Group/private Top-notch video & audio quality;

Recording & Playback;

All-in-One video conferencing equipment for huddle room;

Used on universal platforms including iOS and Android system;

Numerous built-in add-ons;

Free and best screen sharing;

Telephone dail-in supported;

High class meeting control room management system

Security and encryption;

Zoom:

Simultaneous online screen sharing, group messaging and presence;

H.323/SIP room system integration;

MPEG 4 client recording and cloud recording;

Annotation and co-annotation;

Secure Socket Layer (SSL) encryption;

Broadcast to Facebook or YouTube;

Virtual background;

Cloud recording & Playback.

Pros& Cons

Though they are both outstanding video conferencing software with common aspects, they still have their respective strengths and weakness.

ezTalks:

Pros

User-friendly & Mobile-friendly

Security (One-time Password)

As Large as Meeting Capacity

Real-time private and group Chat, Easy sharing and discussing, Useful recording and playback

Seamless Meeting From Desktops and Mobiles (Windows, Mac, iOS, Android-based devices)

Only need Internet to connect

Cons

No API available

Zoom:

Pros

Easy to set up (about 3s from downloading to installing)

Free tier(up to 100 participants)

Industry-specific plans

Customized personal Meeting ID

Unlimited meeting duration for all meeting sizes

Cons

Priced per host

Cloud recording is an add-on with Basic plan

Need Video Conference Codec and Cloud Connector account (paid) to connect

Pricing Plans

Zoom provides four types of pricing plans, including Basic, Pro, Business and Enterprise Plans at the starting price of $14.99/mo/host. Whereas, ezTalks offers three kinds of pricing plans, including Starter Free, Professional and Enterprise Plans at a cheaper starting price of $12.99/mo/host. Both Zoom and ezTalks offer free trial options with the chance of enjoying screen sharing and online meetings.What is worth mentioning is that ezTalks can be joint by telephone call-in and 100mins Webinar free trial is accessible.

User Experience

Users of ezTalks can enjoy the freedom to talk conveniently in front of TV without being tied to their earphone or setting up camera. What's more, different useful functions can be used together with its own software only based on the Internet, which is easy to handle. ezTalks also enables every user to conduct a meeting as a group or as a one on one private meeting. Diversified choices are available. However, the download of Zoom is tiny, less than 10MB in size, winning great favor from the customers. Zoom offers more third-party integration than ezTalks. It's easy to use, but if you need to add more participants, it's a little expensive compared to other applications.

Performance

Both of them are excellent servers to share documents, photographs and videos on your screen simultaneously from anywhere and anytime. Even though you can not be in person (physically) for any situation, you can activate the application online with stereo audio and 1080p HD video resolution vision operation. You can start a meeting with one-click and invite participants with a unique meeting ID. With the help of these two items, you can enjoy smooth meeting controls, like the ability to mute or dismiss participants and to "whiteboard" or annotate while screen sharing. But if you would like to add more people or increase the time limit, Zoom will cost more than ezTalks. With the free trial, you can test them respectively and compare their performance.

Zoho vs Zoom

What is Zoho

Unique and powerful suite of software to run your entire business. It contains word processing, spreadsheets, presentations, databases, note-taking, wikis, web conferencing, customer relationship management, project management, invoicing, and other applications.

What is Zoom

Zoom unifies cloud video conferencing, simple online meetings, and cross platform group chat into one easy-to-use platform

Features

Both of these platforms make it possible to host online meetings. Both allow for voice calling, but Zoom's sound and video quality make the experience feel like all participants are in the same room no matter where they are joining the cloud based meeting from in the world. Both platforms also make it possible for participants to mute their microphone so the rest of the participants do not hear any background noise, but an additional feature with Zoom is the ability of the person leading the meeting to mute and unmute meeting participants. There is also the ability for participants to have a discussion in chat while the online video meeting is going on, or to "raise a hand" so the presenter knows there is a question but not detract from the current conversation taking place.

Ease of Use

Both, Zoom and Zoho are user friendly, making it possible for the user to start hosting online meetings and web conferences right away from your office computer or laptop that is equipped with video and microphone capabilities. However, Zoom really is the better option for those who need to join web meetings while on the go. Unlike Zoho, Zoom is able to be used on a number of Android and iOS based mobile devices, making it possible for your team to meet while travelling or to network from the other side of the world the same way they would if they were working from a centralized location. Share your mobile or smart phone screen, other content, share video live and more with zoom. So whether you are in your office, at home, in an airport, or at a hotel you can participate in online meetings with Zoom. And if you have any trouble connecting, there is support available from both Zoho and Zoom to help answer your questions, but Zoom goes a step further in helping you troubleshoot, by also offering the ability to help remotely.

Price Comparison

While pricing is not the only factor in selecting an online meeting tool, it is often a deciding factor for a number of different companies, especially small businesses with limited budget dollars. Both options offer users a free trial before committing to ensure they are happy with the services offered. However, only Zoom offers an unlimited trial version that gives basic access. The basic access for Zoho then is $12 a month, while Zoom is still FREE. For those who need the additional features offered by the professional membership, Zoho is $18 a month for a host, while Zoom is $14.99 a month for a host. Zoom comes standard with 100 participants in your meeting. Additional multiple user access for larger businesses with Zoho goes up to $49.99 a month, while Zoom goes up to $19.99, making Zoom more economical.

CHAPTER THREE:

HOW TO USE ZOOM LIKE A PRO

Avoid bright red or green colors.

"This is a weird little piece of advice," you might say. The truth is that many devices, no matter how high-end they are, have a tough time with vivid red and green colors on their front-facing cameras. The CMOS behind the lens might make your clothes or background bleed out into each other depending on the lighting situation you find yourself in.

Also – and this is true of all video calls – you should avoid wearing striped clothing that has an excessively vivid contrast, since this might make for a pretty dizzying visual display.

Consider Your Environment

Your surroundings say a lot about you. Let's make sure that they say the right things. Dirty clothes in a pile, an unmade bed, and so forth give the impression that you're not a professional to be trusted with serious work. Clean up and have a simple background (a plain wall, a potted plant, or a bookshelf works perfectly). Zoom also provides virtual backgrounds to help you disguise even the most recklessly cluttered environments.

Lights, camera, action! Note, the first item here is LIGHTS. Position yourself so that most of the light is coming from in front of you (behind your monitor), instead of behind you. If you have a window behind you, shut the blinds. Otherwise, you will be backlit.

Barking dogs and slamming doors are not just annoying in person, they are also annoying via Zoom! Find a quiet space to meet, shut the door, and mute yourself as necessary.

Finding Your Light

The most important and simple thing to remember when setting up your zoom meeting is the light! Spending time designing your space, to sit in the dark won't do you much good. When possible, utilize the natural light around you. Adequate lighting is important but so is color temperature. A mix of warm and cool lighting can throw your video out of whack.

Touch up your appearance

This feels like a good time to remind you that Zoom actually has a feature built in, specifically for the purpose of making you look better. In the Zoom desktop app, there's a "touch up my appearance" option that applies some skin smoothing. It's not perfect, but I know plenty of people who like the fact that it covers up blemishes and gives them a little more of a "ready for primetime" look.

By the way, that feature works better with better lighting. I told you it all comes down to lighting.

Camera

Speaking of camera, the one built into your laptop (especially if it happens to be a MacBook) is pretty much junk. That 720p camera was top-of-the-line back in like, 2010. Now, it's pretty sad really. Do yourself a favor and get something higher quality, especially if you spend a lot of time on camera. I'm a fan of the Logitech 4K Pro

Webcam, which sits right atop my external display and can be adjusted.

Look into the camera.

It can be hard to remember, but this is very important: try to look into your camera, not at yourself, not at the person you're Zooming with. When you look directly into your camera, it will appear, on the other end of your meeting, that you're looking into the eyes of whomever you're Zooming with. Though from time to time it's okay to glance at the images of the people you're meeting with, note that if someone's sitting far away from the camera, it can appear to them that you're looking away from them, not at them. So, every once in a while, during your meetings, try to take note of where you're looking. And if you're not looking into the camera, refocus your gaze.

Positioning

Let's be honest, up the nose is not the best angle for anyone. Instead, your best bet is to have the camera at a height that it can be angled just slightly down at you. Think about the camera as being right at your hairline, and have it pointed down at your eyes. Nothing too extreme, but enough to give you the most flattering angle of view.

While we're talking about positioning, you also don't want to be too close to the camera, or you end up with a distorted face. You may also want to make sure that your camera isn't set to a wide angle, since that has the same effect.

It's okay to get close.

Also very important, and going hand in hand with the above tip, you want to position yourself at a distance from the camera so you're only visible from the shoulders up—think the top third of your body at most. Ideally, you want your face to be the main object of focus. You want people to be able to look into your eyes and see your facial expressions. You also want to see the facial expressions of the people you're meeting with. These visual cues will better mimic in-person conversations, making for better meetings. Although now, in the age of social distancing, you have to keep six feet away from people when you're physically with them, on camera you can be a lot closer (it's okay to be within a foot of the screen). You'll feel a lot different speaking with someone who's closer (but not nose-to-the-camera close) than someone who's sitting or standing far from the camera—so far that you can see their pants as well as their shirt. That distance will make you feel distant from your meeting partners, and that's not ideal.

Headphones

While it's not technically about how you look, how you sound is almost as important. A microphone or good pair of headphones can make a big difference, especially when it comes to reducing background noise.

Share your screen

Share your screen for a Zoom meeting (or to watch a movie or play a game) with other participants by clicking the Share screen icon on the toolbar at the bottom of the meeting screen. You'll have the option to share your entire desktop, or just one of the windows you have open. Click the red Stop Share button at the top of the screen to go back to being a normal participant in the meeting.

Record the meeting to your computer

Both free and paid Zoom subscribers can record their meeting to their laptop or computer using the desktop app (you can't record on mobile at the moment, unless you have a paid account -- keep reading for more on that). Those recorded files can then be uploaded to a file storage service such as Google Drive or Dropbox, or a video streaming service such as YouTube or Vimeo.

To enable local recording, go to Settings > Recording, and toggle it on. When you're hosting a Zoom meeting, click the Record icon on the bottom toolbar

Mute and unmute with the space bar

When you are called on to speak, stop scrambling to click the microphone button. You can press and hold the spacebar to quickly mute and unmute your mic, right from your keyboard.

Mute your audio and turn off your camera by default

Diving for the mute audio and camera buttons as soon as you enter a meeting can get old. Keep your coworkers from seeing your bedhead or hearing your cat screeching by turning those off by default. To do it, go to Settings > Audio > Mute microphone when joining a meeting, and then Settings > Video > Turn off my video when joining a meeting.

Try the Raise Hand Feature

Speaking of having too many people talking at once in a meeting, Zoom also allows users to avoid this issue with hand-raising. Go into the webinar or meeting controls and click on the hand icon to raise your hand. The hand graphic will then appear next to your name on the meeting screen, letting the host know that you want to say something.

This is an excellent way to chime in without being rude if you have something important that you want to discuss with the other people in your team.

React with emoji on screen

If you're muted in a meeting, you can still let the hosts know your thoughts with emoji reactions. Send a thumbs up or a clapping emoji to communicate without interrupting the meeting (by default, those reactions have a yellow skin tone, but you can customize that on the Zoom desktop app).

To react during a meeting, click the Reactions tab at the bottom of the meeting screen (it's in the same panel as mute audio and video, to the right) and choose the one you want. Emoji will disappear after 5 seconds.

If the meeting organizer enables the nonverbal feedback feature, participants can place an icon such as a raised hand next to their name to communicate. Every participant will be able to see each other's feedback.

Prevent embarrassment by silencing desktop notifications

Windows 10 has a built-in feature called Focus Assist that does just this. Just head to Settings > System > Focus Assist, and toggle When I'm duplicating my display to On. You can also toggle it manually from the Action Center found at the bottom right of the Windows 10 taskbar. Mac users need to employ a third-party app to automate the process.

See who attended

Lets say you're using Zoom to hold a mandatory event, like a university lecture or a safety training session. You probably want to know who attends. You can get that information from a report once the meeting is finished.

The attendee list for all meetings lives in the Zoom Account Management > Reports section. Look for Usage Reports, and then click Meeting to find the meeting you want, select the report type and date range, and generate the report.

Requirements: To generate an attendee list, you need to be the 1) the host of the meeting, 2) in a role with Usage Reports enabled, or 3) an account administrator or owner. You also need a Pro, API Partner, Business, or Education plan.

Take advantage of Zoom's powerful scheduling feature

Zoom's built-in scheduling function ties into iCal and Google Calendar, which makes organizing meetings a surprisingly seamless process. The scheduling setup screen even provides some thoughtful options that other videoconferencing services don't, such as the option to start the meeting with video on or off (for both the host and participants), what sort of audio sources to allow, and whether to use your Personal Meeting ID (a dedicated number for your own room) or a randomly generated room number.

Learn a few essential keyboard shortcuts

If you use Zoom more than once a week, there are a couple of keyboard shortcuts worth learning to save you oodles of time.

I is for invite. Press Cmd+I (macOS) or Alt+I (Windows) to jump to the Invite window, where you can grab the link to the meeting or send invitations to others via email.

M is for mute. Press Cmd+Ctrl+M (macOS) or Alt+M (Windows) when you are the meeting host and want to mute everyone else on the line.

S is for share. Press Cmd+Shift+S (macOS) or Alt+Shift+S (Windows) to share your screen.

Mute or unmute audio: Alt + A

Start or stop video: Alt + V

Pause or resume screen sharing: Alt + S

Pause or resume screen recording: Alt + P

Switch camera: Alt + N

Raise or lower hand: Alt + Y

The shortcuts commands are listed for Windows PC users. Mac users will want to substitute the Apple or Command key for the Alt key above.

A full list of the keyboard shortcuts can be found by navigating to the Zoom settings menu and choosing Keyboard Shortcuts on the left pane.

CHAPTER FOUR:

HOW TO AVOID ZOOM-BOMBING

Zoom-bombing is the term for when individuals "gate-crash" Zoom meetings. These uninvited guests share their screens to bombard real attendees with disturbing pornographic and/or violent imagery. Most of these are perpetrated via publicly available Zoom links; however, not all depending on your settings. Here are ways to protect you and your guests from falling victim.

Update Your Zoom Apps

If you want to see that new Security option in your meeting toolbar when you host meetings, you must update our app. Check for and install updates on all devices where you use Zoom.

Set a meeting password

A meeting password — which is automatically generated by Zoom — will prevent uninvited users being able to join your event, even if they have the meeting link. Unfortunately, many Zoombombers swap and obtain meeting codes on social media. Be careful with where you share your meeting code, and if you can, wait to send it out until shortly before the event begins.

Use a Unique ID and Password for Calls

When you create a Zoom account, the app assigns you a Personal Meeting ID (PMI). It's a numeric code that you can give out to people when you want to meet with them. However, you have a second option, which is to generate a unique ID instead of using your PMI. Let me explain how they're different.

The PMI is handy in specific circumstances. It's wonderful for recurring meetings with a small group, like a weekly team meeting or a one-on-one. You can use it over and over, and it never expires, so people can join without having to hunt down this week's login code or link. It's always the same. However, once you give out your PMI, anyone who has it can try to butt into your meetings at any time. If someone knows you're due for a meeting and has your PMI, then it's very easy for that person to crash it.

The unique ID is different every time you schedule a new meeting. As a result, it's inherently more secure.

There's one more layer of security you can add here, a password. Previously, when you scheduled a Zoom meeting, the app would use your PMI and no password by default. Now those settings are swapped. The default is a unique ID with a password, which Zoom generates automatically. You can change that password if you like. You can also choose to add a password to a PMI meeting, and in that case, you must choose your own password, as Zoom will not generate one for you. Once you set a password for PMI meetings, all future meetings will require it, too.

Lock a Meeting Once It Starts

If you start a meeting and everyone you expect to join has, you can lock the meeting from new participants. While the meeting is running, navigate to the bottom of the screen and click Participants. The Participants panel will open. At the bottom, choose More > Lock Meeting.

Use Mute Participants On Entry

You can mute all meeting participants as they enter the meeting. This helps you avoid an unauthorised person coming in and shouting obscenities to disrupt a meeting. The host can unmute the participants as they choose to.

Make Sure Only the Hosts Can Share Their Screen

Don't let anyone hijack the screen during a Zoom call. To prevent it, make sure your settings indicate that the only people allowed to share their screens are hosts. You can enable this setting in advance as well as during a call.

In advance, go to the Zoom web portal (not the desktop app) and in the settings navigate to Personal > Settings > In Meeting (Basic) and look for Screen sharing. Check the option that only the host can share.

During a call, you can use the Security button to change the setting. You can also click the up-facing carrot next to Share Screen and choose Advanced Sharing Options. There, choose to only let the host share.

While sharing your screen or an image, Zoom has a great feature that lets participants annotate what they see. For visual collaboration, it's amazing. For naughty participants, it might seem like an invitation to bomb your call. You can disable the annotation feature in the In Meeting (Basics) section of your web account.

Kick Someone Out or Put Them on Hold

Sometimes an unruly participant manages to slip through the cracks. As the meeting host, you do have the power to kick someone out of a call or put them on hold.

To kick someone out: During the call, go to the Participants pane on the right. Hover over the name of the person you want to boot and when options appear, choose Remove.

By default, an ousted guest cannot rejoin. What to do if you make a mistake? You can allow a booted party to rejoin. Enable this feature by going to the web portal and navigating to Settings > Meeting >

In-Meeting (Basic). Toggle on the setting called Allow removed participants to rejoin.

Alternatively, you can put someone on hold. During the call, find the video thumbnail of the person you want to put on hold. I like to think of it as putting someone in a time-out. Click on their video image and select Start Attendee On Hold. Once they've learned their lesson, you can press Take Off Hold in the Participants panel.

Disable Someone's Camera

Hosts can turn off any participant's camera. If someone is being rude or inappropriate on video, or their video has some technical problem, the host can open the Participants panel and click on the video camera icon next to the person's name.

Make Sure Removed Participants Can't Rejoin

In the settings area of your Zoom meeting, you want to toggle off a setting that says, "Allow removed participants to rejoin." This will ensure anyone you've booted out can't try to get back into your video meeting.

Use Zoom's waiting room feature

This lets you check out everyone before they actually gain access to the meeting. You can then either let them in or not.

When each participant clicks on their link, they will be asked to wait, while you will get a notification telling you that someone has entered the waiting room. You can either immediately admit them or click on "See waiting room."

A sidebar will then show you everyone who is waiting to enter the meeting; you can then either admit them, remove them from the waiting room (and from any chance to enter the meeting), or send them a message.

Having to approve everyone who wants to join might be a pain to deal with, especially if you're expecting a lot of people, but it will ensure that anyone who shows up in your meeting actually belongs there

Restrict other features as needed in host controls

Zoombombers will leverage every feature they can to ruin a meeting. For some meetings it might make sense to block private chats, turn off file transfers and restrict custom backgrounds, all of which could be used to taunt or harass participants.

Set a meeting password

A meeting password — which is automatically generated by Zoom — will prevent uninvited users being able to join your event, even if they have the meeting link. Unfortunately, many Zoombombers swap and obtain meeting codes on social media. Be careful with where you share your meeting code, and if you can, wait to send it out until shortly before the event begins.

Restrict other features as needed in host controls

Zoombombers will leverage every feature they can to ruin a meeting. For some meetings it might make sense to block private chats, turn off file transfers and restrict custom backgrounds, all of which could be used to taunt or harass participants.

Don't publicly share meeting links

This might seem like common sense, but only share meeting links with the people meant to be in the meeting. Don't share them on public platforms like Facebook or Twitter

Require participant authentication

Zoom's authentication feature allows hosts to restrict the participants who can join their meeting to those logged into Zoom. If a participant isn't signed in, or is signed in with an email address different from the one that received the meeting invitation, they won't be able to get in

What To Do If Someone Zoombombs Your Zoom Video Chat

It happened. Despite your careful efforts of prevention, some jackal has gotten into the meeting to cause chaos for kicks. Short of ending the meeting entirely, here are a few things you can do to try and get rid of them.

1. Lock them out. Go to the Participants List in the navigation sidebar, and scroll down to More. Click Lock Meeting to stop further participants from entering the meeting and to be able to remove participants.

2. Shut them up. Have yourself or one of your co-hosts go to the Participants List, again scrolling down to the bottom, and click Mute All Controls. This makes it so the unwelcome participant can't use their microphone to disrupt your audio

CHAPTER FIVE:

MANAGING YOUR PASSWORD

Password requirements

For security purposes, Zoom has a few requirements that your password must meet. These apply when setting your initial password or when resetting your password.

Note that these only apply when using your email address and Zoom password to login to Zoom. If you login with Google, Facebook, or Single Sign-On, your password must meet their requirements.

- Must be at least 8 characters

- Cannot be longer than 32 characters

- Have at least 1 letter (a, b, c...)

- Have at least 1 number (1, 2, 3...)

- Include both uppercase and lower case letters

- Cannot contain only one character (i.e., "111111" or "aaaaaa")

- Cannot contain consecutive characters (i.e., "123456" or "abcdef")

Changing Your Password

You can easily change your Zoom password at any time if you know your existing password.

- Sign in to the Zoom web portal.

- Click to Profile.

- Sign in to the Zoom web portal.

- Scroll down to Sign In Password, Click Edit on the right.

- Enter your Old Password.

- Enter your New Password twice to confirm.

Note: Make sure your password meets the requirements.

- Click Save Changes.

Note: If you do not have the option to change your password on your Profile page, you may only have logged in with Google or Facebook previously.

Adding Password Login To Google Or Facebook Login

If you have previously logged in with Google or Facebook only, on Profile, you will see icons indicating Google or Facebook, but no icon for email. Unless restricted by your Account owner, you can easily add an email and password login for the same account.

- Sign out of your Zoom existing account.

- Go to zoom.us/signup

- Enter in the email address that matches your Google, SSO or Facebook login.

- Click Sign Up.

- You will receive an email with Sign Up instructions. Click to Activate Account.

- Enter your desired password twice.

Note: Make sure your password meets the requirements.

- Click Continue.

You can enter in email addresses of contacts to invite or choose Skip this Step.

- Click Go to My Account.

This will take you to My Profile of the existing Zoom account. It should now show the Google, Facebook or SSO icon that it showed previously, as well as an email icon to indicate that you can login with email address and password.

Forgotten Youur Password

If you have forgotten your Zoom password, you can easily reset it.

Instructions

- Go to Zoom.us/forgot_password

- Enter in your Email address.

- Click Send.

- Enter in your new password.

- Enter in the new password a second time for confirmation.

- Click Save.

- You have now reset your password and should be logged into the Zoom web portal. Click Go to My Meetings to be taken to the web portal.

Password Troubleshooting

Resetting your password

If you login with your email address and password, you can reset your password at zoom.us/forgot_password.

"This Zoom Account Does Not Exist" error message

If you receive a message that states "This Zoom account does not exist", you may have setup an account with Google or Facebook login. Try logging in with Google or Facebook and reset your password with them if necessary.

CHAPTER SIX:

COMMON ZOOM TROUBLESHOOTING STEPS

My Video/Camera Isn't Working

If your camera is not showing up in the Zoom Settings or it is selected and not showing any video, these tips can help you troubleshoot why it is not working.

Troubleshooting Tips For Windows

- Make sure that all other programs that utilize the camera are not using the camera or are closed.

- Restart your computer.

- Uninstall the Zoom client and reinstall the latest version from our Download Center.

- Visit your device's support and downloads page to update the camera driver:

  ➢ Logitech

➢ Dell

➢ Lenovo

➢ HP

➢ ASUS

➢ Samsung

➢ Sony (PC) (Webcams)

Windows 10 has a privacy feature that may block Zoom from using the camera.

Troubleshooting Tips For MacOS

- Make sure that all other programs that utilize the camera, such as Photo Booth and Facetime, are closed.

- Restart your computer.

- If the camera still does not work in Zoom after restarting, check if the camera works in a Mac app, such as Photo Booth or Facetime.

  ➢ If it works elsewhere, uninstall the Zoom client and reinstall the latest version

> ➢ If it does not work in any application, contact Apple support.

Note: If you are on on Mac OS 10.14 Mojave and are still having difficulty accessing the camera, check your operating system permissions to confirm that Zoom has access to the camera.

Troubleshooting Tips For Linux

- Make sure that all other programs that utilize the camera are not using the camera or are closed.

- Restart your computer.

- If it does not work after restarting, uninstall the Zoom client and reinstall the latest version

Troubleshooting Tips For Android Devices

- Attempt to start your video by tapping Video.

- Switch between the front camera and the back camera by tapping Switch Camera.

- Check if any other applications are already using the camera.

  > ➢ Open recent applications. How to open this varies by

devices. On some devices, you can hold down the home button and some have a recent applications key.

➤ Swipe right to close any applications that are using the camera.

- Check that Zoom has permissions for the camera.

  ➤ Open the device Settings.

  ➤ Tap Applications.

  ➤ Tap Application Manager.

  ➤ Tap Zoom.

  ➤ If it does not list access to take pictures and videos, uninstall and reinstall the app as shown below.

- Uninstall and reinstall the Zoom app.

  ➤ Open your device Settings.

  ➤ Tap Applications.

  ➤ Tap Application Manager.

  ➤ Tap Zoom.

  ➤ Tap Uninstall.

  ➤ Confirm Uninstall.

  ➤ Open the Play Store.

  ➤ Search for Zoom Cloud Meetings.

> ➤ Tap Install.

- Restart your Android device.

Troubleshooting Tips for iOS devices

- Attempt to start your video by tapping Start Video.

- Tap the camera icon at the top of your screen to switch between the front and back cameras

- Ensure no other apps are using the camera.

  > ➤ Double tap the home button to view all open apps.

  > ➤ Swipe up on any apps that may be using the camera.

- Confirm that Zoom has camera access.

  > ➤ Open your iOS Settings.

  > ➤ Tap Privacy.

  > ➤ Tap Camera.

  > ➤ Toggle Zoom access to on (green).

- Restart your iOS device.

- Delete the Zoom app and reinstall it from the App Store.

  > ➤ Hold down on the Zoom app icon until it starts to move and an X appears.

➢ Tap the X.

➢ Confirm that you want to delete the app by tapping Delete.

➢ Open the App store.

➢ Search for Zoom.

➢ Tap the cloud next to ZOOM Cloud Meetings to download it.

➢ Once it's finished downloading, Zoom will appear in your apps.

• Confirm that the camera is working in other iOS apps, such as the Camera app.

➢ If it works in other apps, contact Zoom support.

➢ If it does not work in any app, contact Apple support.

Troubleshooting Audio Echo In A Meeting

If you hear audio echo or audio feedback during your meeting, there are 3 possible causes:

• A participant has both the computer and telephone audio active

- Participants with computer or telephones speakers that are too close to each other

- Multiple computer with active audio in the same conference room

Case 1: A participant has both the computer and telephone audio active

If you join from a computer and call in from the telephone, please make sure you either

- Enter your participant ID when calling in, or enter your #participant ID# when already in the call

- Or, manually leave computer audio on your computer

Case 2: Participants with computer or telephones speakers that are too close to each other

If another participant is too close to you, and both of you have speakers on, please leave audio conference on one of the computers or hang up of the the telephone connections.

Case 3: Multiple computer with active audio in the same conference room

If you are in a conference room with multiple devices, please disconnect computer audio from the other devices.

- Select Audio Options > Leave Computer Audio (PC/Mac) or Disconnect (Android/iPhone).

- Muting is not enough as you mute the mic but the speaker is still on.

Other Tips:

Generally, if you are hearing echo, it means that there is a device out there that is channeling your audio back.

To isolate the attendee:

- Host can mute the attendee one at a time

- Host can mute all, and unmute one at a time

- Attendee can mute him/herself

The source of echo can also be from:

- Speakers (such as TV or soundbar) that are too loud

- Echo cancellation has failed (device or performance issue)

- A bad microphone

CHAPTER SEVEN:

ENABLING BREAKOUT ROOMS

Breakout rooms allow you to split your Zoom meeting in up to 50 separate sessions. The meeting host can choose to split the participants of the meeting into these separate sessions automatically or manually, and can switch between sessions at any time.

Limitations

Only the host can assign participants to breakout rooms. The co-host can leave and join any breakout room only if they join a breakout room assigned to them by the host.

Users joined into the Zoom meeting from the Zoom Mobile App or H.323/SIP devices can participate in breakout rooms, but cannot manage them. Users joined using Chromebooks/Chrome OS or Zoom Rooms are unable to join breakout Rooms, but the main room can be used as an alternative session for these users.

If the meeting is being cloud recorded, it will only record the main room, regardless of what room the meeting host is in. If local recording is being used, it will record the room the participant who is recording is in. Multiple participants can record locally.

You can create up to 50 breakout rooms. The maximum number of participants in a single breakout room depends on the meeting capacity, number of breakout rooms created, and if participants are assigned during the meeting or before the meeting.

These numbers only apply to breakout rooms created during a meeting. Up to 200 participants can be pre-assigned to breakout rooms.

Number of breakout rooms	Maximum number of participants who can be assigned to breakout rooms*
20 breakout rooms	Up to 500 participants
30 breakout rooms	Up to 400 participants
50 breakout rooms	Up to 200 participants

The maximum capacities listed require a Large Meeting add-on. If you do not have a Large Meeting add-on, the maximum number of participants is limited by your meeting capacity.

Creating Breakout Rooms

Note: You can also pre-assign participants to breakout rooms when you schedule the meeting instead of managing them during the meeting.

- Start an instant or scheduled meeting.
- Click breakout rooms.
- Select the number of rooms you would like to create, and how you would like to assign your participants to those rooms:
  - ➢ Automatically: Let Zoom split your participants up evenly into each of the rooms.
  - ➢ Manually: Choose which participants you would like in each room.
- Click Create breakout rooms.

- Your rooms will be created, but will not start automatically. You can manage the rooms prior to starting them by following the instructions below.

Options For Breakout Rooms

- After creating the breakout rooms, click Options to view additional breakout rooms options.

- Check any options that you would like to use for your breakout rooms.

  ➢ Move all participants into breakout rooms automatically: Checking this option will move all participants into the breakout rooms automatically. If this option is unchecked, the participants will need to click Join to be added to the breakout room.

  ➢ Allow participants to return to the main session at any time: If this option is checked, the participants can move back to the main session from their meeting controls. If this is disabled, they need to wait for the host to end the breakout rooms.

➢ Breakout rooms close automatically after x minutes: If this option is checked, the breakout rooms will automatically end after the configured time.

➢ Notify me when the time is up: If this option is checked, the host will be notified when the breakout room time is up.

➢ Countdown after closing breakout rooms: If this option is checked, the participants will be given a countdown of how much time they have left before being returned to the main room.

• Follow the steps below to assign participants to rooms or click Open All Rooms to start the breakout rooms.

Assigning Participants To Rooms

To assign participants to your rooms, select Assign next to the room you wish to assign participants to and select participants you want to assign to that room. Repeat this for each room.

Once a participant has been assigned (manually or automatically), the number of participants will show in place of the Assign button.

Preparing Breakout Rooms

After manually or automatically assigning participants to rooms, you can rearrange the participants. Participants who are not assigned to breakout sessions will remain in the main meeting when the rooms are started.

- Move to (participant): Select a room to move the participant to.

- Exchange (participant): Select a participant in another room to swap the selected participant with.

- Delete Room: Delete the selected room.

- Recreate: Deletes existing breakout rooms and creates new ones.

- Add a Room: Add another breakout room.

- Open All Rooms: Start the rooms. All participants will be moved to their respective rooms after confirming the prompt to join the breakout room. The host will be left in the main meeting until manually joining one of the rooms. The participants (and the host when manually joining a room) will see the following message shown when joining the breakout room.

Managing Breakout Rooms In Progress

Once the breakout rooms have been started, the participants will be asked to join the Breakout Session. The host will stay in the main meeting until joining a session manually. If a participant has not joined the session yet, it will be noted by (not joined) next to their name.

- Join: Join the breakout room.
- Leave: Leave the room and return to the main meeting (only shows when in a breakout room).
- Close All Rooms: Stops all rooms after a 60 second countdown, shown to the host and participants, and returns all participants back to the main meeting.

Responding To Requests For Help

Participants in breakout rooms can request that the meeting host join their meeting by clicking Ask for Help.

You will be prompted to join the room where the request originated from. Click Join breakout room to join the room.

Broadcasting A Message To All Breakout Rooms

The host can broadcast a message to all breakout rooms to share information with all participants.

- Click breakout rooms in the meeting controls.

- Click Broadcast a message to all, enter your message and click Broadcast.

- The message will now appear for all participants in Breakout Rooms

Few recommendations to make your nonprofit Zoom (or similar online meeting software like Skype, GoToMeeting) meetings profitable:

1) Develop a six-month digitally based, as opposed to travel based, plan for each segment of your donor base. This can be determined by gift amounts, age, or some other designation that's meaningful to your nonprofit's mission.

2) Give each of these initiatives a title and craft an approach or journey, number of meetings (avoiding donor fatigue), talking points, and value-added inputs reinforcing donors, then build the number of meetings around what works best to keep them informed, enthused, and engaged.

3) Create a template for your invitation, reminder, and follow-up emails, a professional look that presents the nonprofit with its best foot forward.

4) Recognize that donors are learning online meeting software too, so make joining the meeting-linking-as simple as possible, likely not using passwords unless considered absolutely necessary for security.

5) Script the meeting, i.e., don't wing it. Identify theme, presentation points, outcomes desired, action steps, and how long the meeting will last-briefer is generally better.

6) Check lighting beforehand. Better lighting enhances your professional image and impact. Lighting - what lighting technicians call Key (straight on at the speaker), Hair (overhead), and Fill (side) lighting - make the difference between a meeting appearing as if it's

occurring in a studio and one that feels like it's taking place in a tunnel.

7) Check sound beforehand. Using an external microphone almost always

yields a more complete, fuller sound and cuts down on echoes.

8) Determine what backdrop you wish to share behind the host and/or panelist speakers. Is it virtual or do you need to set up a green screen? Does your backdrop overpower the speaker? The backdrop could be the nonprofit organization logo, if this does not distract in some way, or it could be a map or some other image pertinent to your mission.

9) If there's any potential for your WiFi to become unstable, use an ethernet cord to plug your computer directly into your router. This helps reduce delay and interruption.

10) Decide whether recording the meeting is needed and appropriate, and if you record, determine you need to inform participants of this at the top of the meeting.

11) Once your donors join the call, direct them to the upper righthand corner of

their screen and suggest they click Speaker View so they can focus on the person presenting and lessen distractions from others. And tell them about the Chat button at the bottom and how to use it to ask questions.

12) Welcome your guests, thank them for their time, tell them-if this fits your

purposes-that they will be muted to cut down on inadvertent noise from coughing, children, pets, etc.-then Go... being sure to end at the pre-scheduled time.

Five Tips To Insure You Not Only Make A Great Impression,

But That You Also Easily Place Yourself Above Your

Competition.

Zoom Tip #1: Clear away any and all unprofessional distractions. Oh, I know, everyone is working from home so a dog barking or kids screaming in the background should be O.K., right? Wrong. You are a representative of your company, and you are a professional. I wouldn't bring my dog to the office, would you? How about your kids? Of course not. It's key for you to present a professional, confident, and competent image, and that means one free of distractions.

So, get your wife or husband to mind the kids-they are probably at home with you-take the dog outside and shut the door. Create an environment of professionalism.

Zoom Tip #2: Speaking of professionalism, what are you wearing to your Zoom meetings? Because you're confined at home, are you showing up in a tee-shirt or sweatshirt? Or are you wearing business casual and at least wearing a nice button-down shirt?

And if you're a man, have you shaved? Combed your hair? Or do you look like you've just gotten off the couch? If you're a woman, is your hair looking neat? How about make-up, if you wear it?

How you appear makes a huge impression on your clients and prospects. You want to look your best, and it doesn't take much effort. Make it.

Zoom Tip #3: Lighting. Now I know you're not in the film industry, but lighting is crucial to any type of filming. I was on a meeting with someone just the other day and it appeared as if they were calling from a cave. It was so dark, I could barely see them.

And then I've been in meetings with people sitting in front of a sunlit window. Same thing: I couldn't see their face because they were drowned out in shadow.

When considering where to film, make sure you're not too backlit that your face will be dark, and if you're in a dark study or den, then turn the lights on or open your blinds.

You all know how much difference a well shot, well lit film looks compared to a B-film. Remember: Image is everything in front of a camera.

Zoom Tip #4: Background is important as well. Have you ever been on a Zoom meeting with someone and thought, "Ewe, that guy/gal is a slob! Look at that messy couch and bookcase and those crooked pictures. Yuck!"

Ladies and gentlemen, we know your home is your kingdom, and that you'll live any way you choose. And you should. But we don't need to see it all.

If you don't have a professional background, then the solution is simple: Use one of Zoom's greenscreen backgrounds. There are plenty to choose from and you can find even more by Googling "Zoom Background Images."

Oh, I know-if you move too fast then the background blurs. Two things about that: 1) Don't move so much. In fact, if you look at any professional newscaster, they move very little. You should practice that. 2) Everybody expects them to move so you've got some leeway there. Regardless, a background image is almost always better than what you've got going on now...

Zoom Tip #5: Be professional and respectful at all times. That includes:

• Being on time.

• Not speaking over someone.

• Sending an email afterwards thanking them for their time.

You know, all the things you would normally do if you were back at the office.

CONCLUSION

Zoom unifies cloud video conferencing, simple online meetings, and group messaging into one easy-to-use platform.

If you're new to Zoom (and video conferencing in general), it can take some time getting used to. You might even feel hesitant to use Zoom for work meetings, wanting to stay in your comfort zone and keep using the phone, email, and Slack. However, if you give Zoom a try, you'll likely find that there are many benefits to Zoom—and even come to prefer Zooming over your old ways of communicating.

Also, it's important to remember that now is not a normal time. And so, don't be hard on yourself if you're Zooming and your son runs through the room and is visible on camera, or your neighbor's car alarm goes off and won't stop, or your internet connection is so slow that your face freezes. In the time of a global pandemic, doing your best is all that you can do, all anyone can ask of you. People you Zoom with will certainly understand any minor technical difficulties you might experience.

Made in the USA
Middletown, DE
23 October 2020

22566557R10080